THE STORY OF
CHRISTOPHER COLUMBUS,
Admiral of the Ocean Sea

====== THE STORY OF ======
CHRISTOPHER COLUMBUS,
Admiral of the Ocean Sea

BY MARY POPE OSBORNE

ILLUSTRATED BY STEPHEN MARCHESI

A YEARLING BOOK

ABOUT THIS BOOK

This book has been carefully researched from authentic biographies and writings. No part of this biography has been fictionalized. The events described in the book are true.

To learn more about Christopher Columbus, ask your librarian to recommend other fine books you might read.

To Michael Grody

Published by
Dell Publishing
a division of
The Bantam Doubleday Dell Publishing Group, Inc.
666 Fifth Avenue
New York, New York 10103

ISBN:0-440-41275-7

Published by arrangement with Parachute Press, Inc.

Printed in the United States of America
October 1987

10 9 8 7 6 5 4 3 2

CW

Contents

Introduction

DURING THE LIFETIME OF CHRISTOPHER Columbus (1451–1506), the country of Spain was starting to become a powerful nation. In 1492 Spain won its final battle against the Moors in Granada, the last Arab stronghold in Spain. Now Christianity ruled Spain for the first time in many centuries.

King Ferdinand and Queen Isabella of Spain were called the Catholic Kings because they were very religious. They insisted that everyone in their country be a Christian. Many Jews and Moors (as the Moslems in Spain were often called) were forced to become Christians or to leave the country.

Queen Isabella also wanted people all over the world to become Christians. When a sailor named Christopher Columbus promised to spread Christianity to faraway countries, Queen Isabella promised to help him. This began a relationship that would change the history of the world.

Sailor and Mapmaker

IN 1451, IN GENOA, ITALY, SUSANNA CO-lumbus gave birth to a baby boy. She named him after Saint Christopher, the patron saint of travelers. When Christopher Columbus was a child, he always wanted to be like Saint Christopher. He wanted to sail to faraway places and spread the word of Christianity.

Christopher Columbus didn't go to school. In fact, he didn't learn to read or write until he was a grown man. He and his brothers, Bartholomew and Diego, helped their father with his work. Their father, Domenico, was a simple wool weaver. Christopher's grandfather had been a weaver, and his mother was the daughter of a weaver.

But Christopher Columbus did not want to be a weaver when he grew up. He wanted to go to sea. Genoa was a seaport town, so whenever Columbus could find the time, he walked through the narrow cobblestone streets down to the wharves. He liked to watch the big ships come and go. He liked to go fishing, and he liked to talk to the sailors who had just returned from sea journeys.

The ships that docked in Genoa traveled all over the Mediterranean. Columbus would listen to the sailors talk about their trading adventures. He talked with them about storms at sea and about faraway places. Some of the sailors even told about huge monsters deep in the ocean.

Only very ignorant people in those days thought that the world was flat. Most people, including the sailors, knew it was round. But the sailors of Genoa had no idea how big the world was. The Vikings from Scandinavia had probably already visited North America. But historians believe that the news of the Vikings' discoveries of a new continent had never reached southern Europe. So the people of Columbus's world knew nothing about the continents of North America and South America.

When Columbus was older, he sailed up

and down the coast of Italy with his two brothers. The boys sold their father's cloth and bought wine and cheeses. On these trips Columbus learned to find his way through the sea. But he wanted to learn much more about sailing, and he wanted to learn from the finest sailors in the world—the Portuguese. So when he was just thirteen years old, Christopher Columbus left home to become a real seaman.

For many years Columbus worked on trading ships, sailing back and forth across the Mediterranean Sea. The older sailors taught him how to sail through bad storms and strong winds. They told him what to take on long trips and how to trade with natives. And they showed him how to use a compass. At that time sailors depended a great deal on the mariner's compass, which was a circular box containing a magnetic needle that always pointed to the north. The sailors also studied the height of the North Star at night and the position of the sun at noon to help them find their way. And a good sailor knew about birds, fish, drift-

5

wood, seaweed, and the color of the water—all these things helped him figure out where he was.

In 1476, when Columbus was twenty-five years old, pirates attacked the ship he was on, and the ship sank. But Columbus clung to a board in the water and made his way six miles to the nearest Portuguese shore.

After Columbus recovered from the ordeal of the shipwreck, he found out that his brother Bartholomew had a map store in Lisbon, Portugal. Columbus hurried to Lisbon to find Bartholomew. And for the next eight years he worked in the map store with his brother.

The city of Lisbon had a great effect on Columbus. It changed the course of his life—and, consequently, the course of history. Lisbon was a lively, bustling seaport town and also a center for learning. Columbus studied different languages and read many books about the world.

In Lisbon, Columbus met and then married a woman named Dona Felipa. They had a son named Diego. Dona Felipa was from a noble family. Her father had been a

sailor and explorer, and Columbus loved talking with him about his explorations and travels.

Lisbon, at that time, was also a great center for discovery and exploration. Sailors no doubt came into Columbus and Bartholomew's map store to discuss their thoughts about the size and shape of the earth. The Portuguese explorers were getting better and better at ocean travel. Many of them were sailing north and south, trying to find new trade routes to the Indies. The Indies meant Eastern Asia—the countries of China, Japan, India, Indonesia, and Burma.

The explorers wanted spices from these countries. They also wanted gold, jewels, silks, and pearls. For a while traders had traveled over land to get to the Indies. They had to go through the country of Turkey if they went overland. But in 1453 the Moslem Turks had defeated the Christian armies of Constantinople, a large city in Turkey. And now the Turks did not allow the traders to pass through their country to get to Asia. The only route left to the European traders was by sea. So many explorers were now trying to sail around Africa to find a way to the Indies.

While working together Christopher and Bartholomew began to have their own ideas about how to get to the Indies. Columbus had been eager to see the Indies ever since he'd read a book by a man from Venice, Italy, named Marco Polo. Marco Polo had traveled over land to Eastern Asia more than two hundred years before. His book told about the Great Khan of China and the golden rooftops of Japan.

Columbus wondered what would happen if he sailed west across the Western Ocean. (Today we call that Western Ocean the Atlantic.) Wouldn't he come to Eastern Asia? Wouldn't this be a much shorter trip than going all the way around Africa? Of course, Columbus did not know that North America, South America, and the Pacific Ocean were in between!

No explorers during Columbus's time had yet tried to sail across the Western Ocean. Many called this ocean "the Sea of Darkness." They didn't try to sail across it because they didn't know how big it was. They thought it would take too many years to get to the Indies, and they were afraid of running out of supplies. They were also afraid that a ship could not sail back. Since the world was round, wouldn't the ship sail *downhill* going one way? And then have to sail *uphill* coming back?

Christopher Columbus was not afraid to sail across the Western Ocean. Some people thought he was crazy, but he was sure that he could find a quick western route to the Indies. When he was thirty-three years old, the sailor and mapmaker began planning for his trip across the Sea of Darkness.

The Long Wait

FIRST COLUMBUS NEEDED MONEY TO PAY for his men and ships, so he decided to find a king to help him. The first king he went to see was King John II of Portugal.

King John II was very interested in finding a sea route to the Indies. His great-uncle, Henry the Navigator, had founded the world's first school of navigation in Portugal. For a long time the Portuguese sailors and explorers from Henry the Navigator's school had been trying to sail around Africa to get to the Indies.

In 1484 Columbus spoke with King John and told him that he wanted to sail across the Western Ocean to find the Indies. He showed the king many things to prove that his plan would work. He showed him letters from a famous geographer named Toscanelli, who believed that Japan could be reached by sailing west. He showed him quotes from the Bible to prove that the ocean was not very big. He told the king about rare fruit that washed up on a shore near Spain. Fruits such as these could only come from the Indies! And he told the king about bodies that had been found in the sea—bodies with faces like the people of the Indies!

Didn't all this prove that the Indies were not really very far away? If King John would help him, he promised to bring back great riches for Portugal.

King John thought Columbus was a big talker and very boastful. Still, he seriously thought about Columbus's plan. He even asked his advisers to study it.

But King John's advisers said no—absolutely not. Columbus's plan would never work, they said. The distance across the ocean was much greater than Columbus thought it was. They said that King John should keep trying to sail around Africa to get to Eastern Asia.

King John's refusal was no doubt a big disappointment to Columbus. However, something worse happened. His wife, Dona Felipa, died. Columbus had no more reason to stay in Portugal. His wife was gone and gone were his hopes for support from King John. So Columbus packed his things, and he and his five-year-old son, Diego, left for Spain.

When they arrived in the seacoast town of Palos, Spain, Columbus took Diego to the La Rábida monastery, where the young boy could be raised and educated by Franciscan monks. The monastery was just a simple white building overlooking the water, but it turned out to be an important place for Columbus. Some of La Rábida's monks were scholars of astronomy. They were very interested in Columbus's theories about sailing across the Western Ocean to find the Indies. They even offered to help him. One monk wrote to a nobleman to ask for money for Columbus's trip across the ocean.

The nobleman said yes, he would help, and he offered to give Columbus four ships. But then the nobleman asked Queen Isabella of Spain if that plan was all right with her, and Queen Isabella said no! She said that she and King Ferdinand should be the ones to help Columbus.

So in May 1486 Columbus went to see Queen Isabella and King Ferdinand. At that time the court was residing in the Spanish city of Cordoba. Cordoba was to become Columbus's adoptive city in Spain. It had been an Arab city at one time, and in many ways it still looked like one. The sunny streets were silent and narrow, and at the center of the city was a great Christian cathedral that had once been an Arab mosque.

At the royal court Columbus told the king and queen about his plan to sail across the ocean. He promised to bring back gold and spices for Spain. And he promised to spread Christianity to the people of the Indies.

Queen Isabella was very interested in what Columbus said. She liked his enthusiasm and great imagination, and she was especially excited about his promise to spread Christianity—for this was the subject closest to her heart.

Queen Isabella told Columbus that she

would like to help him, but he must wait until Spain won its war against the Moors in Granada. All the money from the royal treasury was being poured into that war. Isabella promised to help Columbus after the war was won—and all of Spain was under Christian rule.

Columbus settled down in Cordoba to wait for the queen's help. He had no idea he would have to wait six unhappy years before she would see him!

While he was living in Cordoba, Columbus fell in love with a young woman named Beatrice Enriquez de Harana. In August of 1488 Beatrice gave birth to Columbus's second son, Fernando. Beatrice had a lot of faith in Columbus and gave him much support during these hard years of trying to raise the money for his trip to the Indies.

After three restless years of waiting for the Spanish queen and king to help him, Columbus decided to go to Portugal again and ask King John for help. King John wrote to Columbus and told him to come back and discuss his plan once more. He even promised that Columbus would not be arrested for leaving behind all his unpaid bills in Lisbon!

But before Columbus could talk to King John, the king lost interest in him. The Portuguese explorer Dias had recently succeeded in sailing around the tip of Africa! King John no longer cared about finding a route to the Indies across the Western Ocean.

Meanwhile, Columbus's brother Bartholomew went to England and France to try to get help for Columbus. Bartholomew was in France when Columbus decided to give up on Spain. In 1491 he went to the La Rábida monastery to get his son Diego and take him to France.

But the monks at La Rábida told Columbus to wait and try to get Queen Isabella's help again. After all, Spain was just about to win the long war in Granada. The king and queen were camped outside Granada in Sante Fe, a city the Spanish Army had built as they waited for the end of the war. The monks tried to convince Columbus that he should delay his departure from Spain until the war was over. One of the monks wrote to the queen's priest, asking him to try to seek help for Columbus.

The queen finally replied yes. Yes, she would help Columbus! And she asked him to come to the royal camp of Sante Fe. She even sent money to him so he could buy some clothes and a mule for the trip.

Columbus bought his mule, said good-bye to the helpful monks of La Rábida, then headed for Sante Fe. On the way he crossed lands that were wasted by war. But when he arrived at the royal camp of Sante Fe, he found a full bustling city that Spanish soldiers had built in less than three months. Santa Fe had stone walls and towers surrounded by a huge moat. Several thousand people lived in the many buildings inside the fort. Columbus passed through a gate and was led to the royal palace.

He stood before Ferdinand and Isabella and told them what he wanted. First he wanted a noble title: He wanted to be called admiral. In fact, he wanted to be called Admiral of the Ocean Sea! Not only that, but he asked to be governor general of all the lands he might find, and he insisted that title be passed to his first-born son, Diego, after he died. He also demanded ten percent of all the riches he might find—including gold, silver, and jewels!

King Ferdinand said absolutely not! The royal couple thought Columbus's demands were unreasonable. They tried to get Columbus to change his mind, but he wouldn't. He even lost his temper and flew into a rage when they refused him.

Columbus was so driven by his dream of finding the East that he seemed not to care whether he pleased the king and queen. Even when they told him his requests were unreasonable, he refused to give in. In fact, he got back on his mule and left the royal camp of Santa Fe. He was going to France, he decided. He would find his brother Bartholomew, and they would talk to the French king. He would do the trip his way—or not at all!

Meanwhile, advisers to Ferdinand and Isabella talked them into changing their minds. The king and queen sent a messenger

19

running after Columbus to tell Columbus to return to the royal camp so that they "could conclude the affair." A few miles outside of Sante Fe, the messenger spotted Columbus crossing a bridge and gave him the message.

The Admiral of the Ocean Sea happily turned his mule around and rode back to see Queen Isabella of Spain.

Setting Sail

IN APRIL 1492 ALL THE CONTRACTS BETWEEN the king and queen and Columbus were signed. Columbus wanted to set sail before winter came, so he began to gather men for his trip.

First he chose a sailor named Pinzón to be one of his captains. Pinzón was considered to be the best seaman in the area. He was wealthy and came from a family of fine navigators. Although Columbus respected Pinzón for his skill, he did not like his arrogance. Columbus may have been a bit wary of Pinzón. Could Pinzón be trusted? Would he follow orders? Columbus had his doubts.

But for now Columbus needed Pinzón's help to find sailors for the journey. The well-known seaman went around to the taverns by the port and told all the men to come sailing with him and Columbus. He promised the men houses with roofs of gold! He promised fame and glory! Finally ninety men, mostly Spaniards, signed up for the voyage.

Next Columbus prepared three ships— the *Pinta,* the *Niña,* and the *Santa María.* The *Niña* was the smallest—she was only about sixty-five feet long. The *Pinta* was the fastest. And the *Santa María* was the largest—she was over eighty feet long. Columbus sailed on the *Santa María.*

Columbus took cats aboard to kill rats. He took a translator to speak Arabic because he thought the natives in the Indies might speak that language. He packed firewood and compasses, water and wine. He also took weapons, such as cannons, muskets, and crossbows. And the ships carried many foods: sea biscuits, salt, meat, cheese, raisins, beans, honey, rice, almonds, sardines, anchovies.

Columbus also took gifts to give to the people of the Indies. There were bells, scissors, knives, coins, beads, needles, pins, and mirrors.

King Ferdinand and Queen Isabella gave Columbus three letters to take to the Indies.

One letter was for the king of China, the Great Khan. The other two contained blanks for the names of rulers to be filled in.

Columbus left his sons, Fernando and Diego, in a school in the city of Cordoba. Then on the night of August 2, 1492, he and his crew gathered at the little port of Palos. The sailors wore red wool caps as the Admiral of the Ocean Sea led them to church.

The crew prayed for a safe trip, and they vowed to obey their admiral's commands. Then they set sail before daybreak on a perfectly calm sea.

What was it like living on one of Columbus's ships? The *Santa María* was painted red and black. She had a narrow deck with ropes, masts, sails, pumps, and kegs. Cooking was done over a wooden firebox, and the men ate mostly stews (*cocidos*) with small amounts of meat and garbanzo or *haba* beans.

Columbus's cabin was small and contained a canopy bed, a table, and a chest with maps in it. On three walls there were small windows. Below his cabin was a small room for one or two officers.

The other sailors slept in their clothes in whatever space they could find. The ship's boy had the job of keeping time. Every half hour he turned a glass of sand. Then he wrote down the time.

Every half hour the ship's boy also sang out a prayer. The sailors worshiped God a great deal. In the morning, they gathered to hear the ship's boy sing,

"Blessed be the light of day
And the Holy Cross, we say."

Then the boy said two prayers. After sunset, everyone gathered again for more prayers.

After the ships left Palos, the north wind carried them to the Canary Islands off Spain. There they stopped to make some repairs on the *Pinta*. Then on September 6, 1492, the wind and tides carried the three ships into the Western Ocean.

It was a scary moment for many of the sailors. When they had sailed before, they had never been far from shore. But Columbus told them not to worry. He thought it would take just a short time to cross the

24

ocean. He had no idea it would actually take sixty-nine days!

At first the sailing was perfect. For ten days the ships had a calm sea with steady eastern winds. Each dawn was beautiful, and the sails were always full. The sailors saw many fish in the warm ocean waters. And many birds—herons, sea eagles, and sea swallows—followed the ships.

Columbus kept the ships on a westward course. He thought that they sailed about one hundred and forty miles a day. He used maps and compasses, and he studied the stars. But he also guessed a lot at the distance and direction. What is most amazing about Columbus is that his estimated distances were never far off the mark. To this day Columbus is considered to have been a truly great sailor. One of his crew later wrote: "There has been no such great-hearted man or keen navigator as the Admiral. He could tell from a cloud or a single star what direction to follow."

Each day Columbus wrote in a journal how many miles the ships traveled. In another journal he wrote down fewer miles, and he showed this journal to his men to fool them. He was afraid that if they saw how many miles they had actually sailed, they might want to turn back.

Even without knowing the real mileage, the sailors began wanting to return to Spain. They had not seen land for many days, and the sea was starting to seem endless. The sailors were scared when a comet shot through the sky, and they were scared when their food and water became stale.

After about three weeks of ocean travel, the ships ran into a giant bed of seaweed! Green and yellow weeds covered the ocean as far as the men could see. The ships' sails went limp. Then the compass no longer pointed to the North Star. Nowadays sailors do not expect the magnetized compass needle to work perfectly all the time, but in those days the sailors did. And they were very frightened.

But Columbus told his men not to worry. He promised that the ships would move out of the giant beds of seaweed. And they did—finally. But the men were still afraid, and they begged Columbus to turn back.

Columbus wouldn't turn back, though. He wrote in his journal that it was "useless (for his sailors) to complain." He said he had made up his mind to sail to the Indies, and that's what he would do! Columbus often did not care what other people thought. He believed that it was only important to do what God wanted him to do—and he believed that God wanted him to discover a new route to the Indies. Another amazing thing about Columbus was his unswerving religious faith.

The sailors, though, continued to grow more and more fearful and were eager to get off the ships. They were always looking out for land. Furthermore, the first person to see land had been promised a reward from the king and queen of Spain.

Finally, on September 25, 1492, Pinzón, the captain of the *Pinta*, yelled, "Land!" The crew was very excited. Columbus fell to his knees and thanked God. Then he ordered his men to sing a hymn.

But the next day the sailors discovered there was no land. They had only seen a line of clouds lying close to the horizon.

On October 7 the *Niña* fired a cannon. *Land* again! The sailors raised a flag and cheered. But again there was no land. Another false alarm.

Every day the men cried "Land!"

Columbus was angry because there were so many false sightings. He said anyone who again cried *land* falsely would not get the reward even if he was the first to see land later.

On October 10 the men told Columbus they absolutely wanted to turn back. He pleaded with them to give him just three more days.

The next day there were some very hopeful signs of land. The sailors found a carved stick in the water and a branch with buds and flowers. They also saw flocks of birds flying southwest over the mast.

Columbus changed his course. Every day he had said to go *west*. This day he said to go *southwest*. He wanted to follow the birds.

That night Columbus told his men not to drop anchor. He said, *"Adelante!"* Sail on! He promised a silk jacket to the first person who saw land.

At ten o'clock that night, when Columbus

was standing on the deck of his ship, he thought he saw a light flicker near the horizon. It was like the flicker of a wax candle. Then the light went away. But Columbus told his men to drop anchor.

At two o'clock in the morning a sailor named Rodrigo began shouting, "Land ho! Land ho!"

The *Pinta* fired a cannon.

This time there really was land. All the sailors came on deck and saw white cliffs in the moonlight.

The men were so happy to finally be near land that they sang and prayed and cried for joy. They had no idea where they were. But at least their long sea journey was over. It was October 12, 1492.

The New World

AT DAWN THE SAILORS SAW A WHITE beach in the early light. They saw many bright green trees against the sky. There were no signs of people, though. The natives were hiding behind the trees. They were afraid of these three huge monsters. Were they strange fish? Giant birds? Or just houses on top of the water?

The men could not land, because some big rocks were close to the beach. So they sailed to a small bay, and then they went ashore.

Christopher Columbus carried the royal flag of Spain onto the beach. The captains of the *Pinta* and the *Niña* followed with their ships' banners. All the sailors fell to their knees and thanked God for their safe trip.

Columbus placed the flagpole into the sand. He claimed the land for the Spanish king and queen. Then he set a large cross into the ground and named the island *San*

Salvador, which in Spanish means "Holy Savior."

The sailors begged Columbus to forgive them for being scared during the voyage. They all wept and hugged one another.

Meanwhile, the islanders were watching these strange actions from behind the trees. Finally they crept out. They had gold rings in their noses, and their bodies were painted red, black, and other colors. They just stared at the mysterious white men.

The natives seemed to understand that Columbus was the leader of the group. So they went up to him and touched his beard. They touched his red clothes and his white hands. The people of San Salvador had never seen white men before. They thought these were gods who had dropped from heaven.

Columbus thought that the natives were people of the Indies, so he named them Indians. He wrote about them in his journal. He said they were very peaceful people, that they were very handsome, but their hair was like horsehair. He thought they could easily

be brought under control and that they had no religion of their own. He wrote that they would make "good Christians and good servants."

The Indians gave the sailors cotton, parrots, and food. Columbus and his men gave the Indians bells and red caps. They also gave them glass beads, which the Indians wore around their necks. The Indians were curious about the swords that the Spaniards carried. They reached out to touch them and cut themselves on the sharp edges. This impressed the Indians. They had no weapons made of iron. They only had wooden spears with fish teeth at the end.

Columbus and his men spent a couple of days exploring San Salvador. They discovered it to be a large, flat island with very green trees and a big lake. They saw no animals, though, except for parrots and other birds.

Since Columbus believed he had found the Indies, he decided that San Salvador was an island off of China. He was eager to begin looking for gold and spices, so he used sign language to ask the Indians where the gold rings in their noses came from.

The Indians tried to answer back with sign language. Columbus thought they were telling him to go south. He thought they were saying that a king in the south had large vessels of gold.

Two days after they had arrived, Columbus and his men left San Salvador to look for the island of gold. They also wanted to look for Japan. They were certain they had come to the lands that Marco Polo had written about.

From October 14 to October 28, 1492, the three ships sailed among many green islands. Columbus planted crosses on all of them and gave them names.

At first the natives thought the sailors had come from heaven. Many of them ran away and hid. But then they overcame their fear and swam out to the ships. They brought parrots and cotton thread to the sailors. And the sailors gave the natives anything they could lay their hands on. They even gave them bits of broken glass.

When the sailors went ashore, they saw huts made of tree branches with roofs of palm leaves. They ate fruit and grass and drank fresh rainwater from wells. There was no meat to eat because there were no animals, such as goats or sheep, on the islands.

In his diary Columbus wrote that the Indians seemed to live off fish, birds, and crabs. The Indians surprised the Spaniards by also eating large spiders and white worms! But Columbus wrote that the natives were such healthy people, they didn't even have headaches.

Everywhere he went, Columbus asked about gold. The natives told him about a place called Babeque that had lots of gold. Babeque was actually an imaginary place of the Indians. But the Spaniards thought it was real, so they kept looking for it.

As they sailed, Columbus and his crew didn't find Babeque. But they saw fish of many colors. They saw Indians using hammocks for beds, and they saw palm trees and dogs that never barked.

The Spaniards also saw something that

would someday bring their country a lot of money. The Indians were taking puffs on strange torches. For the first time the sailors were seeing people smoke cigarettes. Within a hundred years the people in Europe would be doing the same thing.

As the sailors traveled, they discovered human skulls and bones. The Indians told them about cannibals that had attacked the islands. Columbus believed these cannibals must have been Chinese pirates.

Columbus was actually chasing after two dreams. One was gold, the most precious metal in the world, and the other was the Indies—especially, the countries of China and Japan. What Columbus was seeing did not seem at all like Marco Polo's Indies. But he tried very hard to believe that it was.

On October 28, 1492, the Spaniards stopped on the island of Cuba. Columbus thought he had finally found China. He sent forth several men to find the court of the Great Khan. But when the men came back, they reported finding only fifty huts and one thousand naked people.

For five weeks the three ships sailed among the islands. The Spaniards kept looking for gold and for proof that they had found the Indies.

On December 6 Columbus and his men landed on Haiti. Haiti would become the most important of all the islands to Columbus. Here he would find his first gold, build his first cities, and plant his first seeds.

When the sailors landed in Haiti, they were attacked by swarms of mosquitoes. The mosquitoes were so thick that Columbus named the area the Bay of the Mosquitoes.

But Haiti was a beautiful green island. It had many trees and mountains. And it reminded everyone of Spain. Some of the native women even looked Spanish. The fish resembled Spanish fish, and the trees were similar to the Spanish oak and apple trees. When the days became chilly, it seemed like the winter weather of Spain. Columbus said Haiti was a "large and splendid island." He named it *Hispaniola,* meaning little Spain.

At first the natives on Hispaniola fled from the sailors. But Columbus's Indian guide ran after them and told them that the Spaniards came from heaven. So the natives returned. They gave food to the sailors and kissed their hands and feet.

In November the *Pinta* was separated from the other two ships during a storm at sea. Actually, Pinzón, the captain of the *Pinta*, had decided to set out on his own expedition to look for gold. Columbus suspected this and was very troubled. He was afraid that Pinzón would find gold, then hurry back to Spain and claim all the glory for himself. But Columbus could do nothing about the disappearance of the *Pinta*, so he led his other two ships on through the islands.

On December 24, 1492, the *Niña* and *Santa María* were sailing near the north side of Hispaniola. They were sailing at night because the breezes were better.

Columbus had not slept in two days and was very tired. So he left someone else in charge of the ship and went to his cabin to sleep.

It was such a calm night, the sailor in charge decided to sleep, too. So he left the

Santa María in care of the ship's boy. The ship's boy was just a twelve-year-old—certainly not an expert at sailing.

Suddenly, around midnight, the *Santa María* ran into a coral reef! Columbus later wrote, "The boy felt the rudder drag, heard the sound, and started to scream."

Columbus jumped on deck. He yelled orders to all the sailors: *"Save the ship!"* But the *Santa María* began to leak. Then she started to sink. All the sailors had to leave the ship. They crowded onto the deck of the *Niña* and watched the *Santa María* fall over onto her side.

At dawn the crew tried to take all the cargo off the *Santa María*. Early Christmas morning Columbus wept over his lost ship.

The native chief of Hispaniola, whose name was Guacanagari, also wept when he saw Columbus and his men in so much trouble. He sent large canoes to help the sailors unload the *Santa María*. With the help of the natives the sailors were able to save everything on board. Columbus wrote that "not even so much as a piece of string was missing." He also said that the kind Indians "love their neighbor as themselves."

The Indians helped the sailors save the wood from the *Santa María*. Then Guacanagari put the Spaniards up in his houses. Columbus thanked the kind chief by giving him a shirt and a pair of gloves.

The natives wanted to make the Spaniards feel happy again, so they brought them some gold. Columbus began to believe that somewhere on the island was a big gold mine. His sorrow turned to hope. Perhaps God had wanted his ship to sink. Perhaps God wanted him to build a fort on Hispaniola—and to build it out of the wood from the *Santa María*! And to collect gold from the island!

Columbus grew happy, thinking about God's new plan for him. He decided that he would leave some men behind to build the fort and sail back to Spain to get more supplies and ships to bring back to the Indies.

He chose thirty-nine men to stay and live on Hispaniola. He chose carpenters, a doctor, a tailor, and others needed to make a set-

41

tlement. He left the men with trading goods, food, and weapons.

Columbus told the settlers to take timber from the *Santa María* and to build a fort with a tower and a wide moat. He ordered them to dig cellars to store a year's supply of wine, bread, and grain. He also instructed the men to stock their fort with gold while he was gone. And he promised to come back later to pick it up.

Before he left, Columbus named the new fort *La Navidad*, which in Spanish means Christmas.

A Hero Returns

ON JANUARY 4, 1493, THE *NIÑA* STARTED for home. Two days later the ship came across the *Pinta*. Pinzón, the captain of the *Pinta*, gave excuses for abandoning Columbus. He said that his ship had gotten lost in a fog. Columbus didn't believe him. But he chose not to accuse Pinzón of mutiny, because many of his other sailors were Pinzón's friends and relatives.

The *Pinta* and the *Niña* headed toward Spain together. At first the sailing was smooth; the sea quite calm. But one day, after about six weeks, scary things began to happen. Columbus wrote about them in his journal. He said, "The sea began to swell and the sky grew stormy."

Suddenly a terrible hurricane hit. Huge waves tossed the two ships about like little toys. The wind blew the *Pinta* away from the

Niña's sight. All night Columbus flashed lamps to the other ship! The *Pinta* answered faintly, but then its signals stopped. Columbus and his men thought the *Pinta* had sunk.

The storm raged for three days and three nights. The sailors of the *Niña* were terrified. All they could do was pray. They begged God to save them. They even promised to march barefoot to a shrine of the Virgin Mary the first chance they got.

During the storm Columbus was very sad. He believed he would never see his sons again. He thought his men were about to die, and he thought he would not live to tell about his amazing journey to the Indies.

While his ship was being tossed about, Columbus wrote a letter outlining his trip, and he put the letter in a barrel and dropped it into the sea. He hoped the waves would carry the barrel ashore.

The letter in the barrel was never found, and fortunately, it wasn't needed. The storm passed, and the *Niña* was safe again. As it turned out, the *Pinta* was also safe, but the two ships did not meet up again for the rest of the trip.

A couple of days after the storm the *Niña* dropped anchor off the Azore Islands near Portugal. Columbus and his crew needed to rest from their ordeal. Some of his men wanted to go to a shrine of the Virgin Mary to thank God for saving them, so they took a little boat ashore and began walking in their bare feet to a shrine. But on their way they were arrested by Portuguese soldiers! The sailors explained that they had just come from the Indies, but the soldiers didn't believe them.

The governor of the island sailed out to see Columbus, who was still aboard the *Niña*. Columbus yelled at the governor, demanding his men back. He shouted, "I am the Admiral of the Ocean Sea and viceroy of the Indies, which belong to the Spanish crown!"

The governor laughed. He said no admiral ever sailed such a small ship! But Columbus shouted he was an admiral returning from the Indies. He said that Spain would punish Portugal if his sailors were not set free. Finally the governor gave Columbus his men, and the *Niña* sailed on.

Meanwhile, the *Pinta* was hurrying back to Spain. Pinzón wrote a letter to King Ferdinand and Queen Isabella, asking permission to tell them about the voyage in person. He was very unhappy when he received their letter, saying that Columbus was the man they wanted to see. Pinzón was also quite sick by this time. When the *Pinta* docked, he dragged himself home and died soon after. Some say he died of a broken heart because he knew he would not get the honors that Columbus would soon get.

All of Spain was waiting for Christopher Columbus. On March 15, 1493, after seven months and eleven days, he sailed into Palos, the little port where his trip had begun.

When he landed, Columbus was treated like a great hero. He was honored at many feasts and parades. King Ferdinand and Queen Isabella were waiting for him in Barcelona. He wrote to them about his trip. From that time on Columbus signed all of his letters with a mysterious signature. It looked like this:

.S.
.S.A.A.
X M X
:Xpo FERENS./

No one is exactly sure what this code means, but it seems to combine both Latin and Greek initials, and perhaps means, "I am Christopher, servant of the Most High Saviour, Christ, Son of Mary—"

King Ferdinand and Queen Isabella wrote back to Columbus, telling him to hurry to their court! They couldn't wait to see him!

It was spring as Columbus traveled over the great rolling plains of Spain. The trees were full and green. The fields were ripe with grain.

People cheered Columbus wherever he went. He showed them the parrots, fruits, and golden rings he'd brought back. He showed them amber, cotton, and herbs.

But the crowds were most interested in the six half-naked Indians that Columbus had brought back. Some of the Spanish peasants along the way even tried to pinch the Indians to see if they were real!

Columbus arrived in Barcelona a month after he had landed in Spain. Someone who was there later wrote, "The court and the entire city went outside to welcome the Admiral!" The whole city was decorated for his arrival.

Ferdinand and Isabella waited for Columbus in the courtyard of their palace. The courtyard was full of princes and noblemen, and everyone clapped and shouted as Columbus entered the gate. Flags waved in the April sun.

The king and queen went inside the Great Hall. They sat on their thrones under a canopy of gold.

Columbus followed. Smiling, he climbed steps to them, and they rose to their feet. He kissed their hands. Then they asked him to sit with them—which was a very rare honor.

For more than an hour the king and queen asked Columbus many questions. The Admiral of the Ocean Sea told them all about his voyage. He told about the beautiful green islands and the naked natives.

Columbus gave the royal couple brightly colored parrots and belts made of fish bone.

49

He passed around trays with gold objects on them. Then he presented the six painted Indians. The Indians were later baptized, and Ferdinand and Isabella became their godparents.

Everyone went together into the king's chapel to offer thanks. Someone who was there later said that tears came down the admiral's face as he prayed.

After giving thanks, the king and queen hosted a private dinner for Columbus. The king tasted Columbus's dinner first to make sure it was safe to eat. This was a custom done only for royalty.

The next day King Ferdinand gave Columbus an even greater honor—he asked him to ride around Barcelona with him in the royal carriage. No one, except a relative of the king, had ever been invited to do this.

As Columbus rode around Barcelona with King Ferdinand, the crowds cheered the great hero.

Sadly, these were to be Columbus's greatest days of glory. Life would never be this happy again.

Disaster in Hispaniola

NEWS TRAVELED FAST ABOUT COLUMBUS'S discovery. People were very excited about the gold and the Indians. Everyone believed Columbus had found the Indies. One man in the Spanish court did not believe this, however. And in a letter to a friend, he called Columbus's land "the New World."

But the Pope, the leader of the Catholic church, believed Columbus had found the Indies, and he said that all the lands that Columbus settled would belong to Spain. For this reason King Ferdinand and Queen Isabella wanted Columbus to go back and settle more land as soon as possible. They were also eager for him to bring back lots of gold and spices for Spain.

So Columbus immediately began to prepare for his second trip. This time everyone wanted to sail with him. They all wanted to find gold. Columbus told the men that they could look for gold—but they must also work on the land and plant crops.

Within five months, Columbus was ready to sail again. He had seventeen ships and twelve hundred men! He also took many horses, sheep, cows, goats, pigs, and chickens. He took seeds and grapevines to plant. He took enough wine to last two years, and he took many tools and weapons.

Columbus gave his captains sealed directions on how to get to Navidad. He told them not to look at the directions unless they got separated from the other ships. He wanted to be the only one who knew how to get there.

On Monday, October 7, 1493, the admiral and his seventeen ships set sail. It was a very easy voyage. There was good weather the whole way. The trip took less than a month.

First the fleet came to some new islands. But Columbus wanted to return quickly to his men at Navidad, so he ordered the ships to keep sailing.

On November 27 the ships got close to Navidad. They sent up signals. The fort did not answer. The ships fired their cannons. The fort did not fire back. No canoes came forward to greet the Spaniards. The men on the ships were afraid something terrible had happened. Someone who was on board later wrote, "A sadness and profound grief seized their hearts."

It was almost dark, so the sailors did not go ashore. Columbus ordered the ships to drop their anchors for the night.

The next morning the sailors set foot on Navidad. The fort had been burned to the ground. There were no signs of the Spaniards.

Guacanagari, the chief of Hispaniola, told Columbus that some of the settlers of Navidad had fought among themselves over Indian women and gold. Some were killed during these fights. The other settlers were slain by another tribe of Indians who were angry with the Spaniards for taking their women. Guacanagari claimed that he and his men had tried to help the Spaniards—he himself had even been wounded!

Many of Columbus's men did not believe Guacanagari, and they wanted to punish

him for the loss of the Spaniards. But Columbus did believe him. This was the same chief who had helped him when the *Santa María* had sunk. Columbus forgave him now. He even invited Guacanagari and his men to come aboard his ships. The Indians were terrified of the horses on the ship, though. They'd never seen such animals before. They were afraid the horses would eat them!

The massacre at Navidad marked a turning point in the relationship between the natives and the Spaniards. The joyful harmony the two had shared on Columbus's first trip was now over.

Columbus decided not to settle in Navidad—he thought it was an unlucky place. He chose a new area on Hispaniola and named it Isabella.

But Columbus's men were not happy there. The mosquitoes in Isabella carried the disease malaria, which causes very high fever and chills. The warm humid climate and the native food also made the men sick. After they ran out of their own food, they did not want to plant crops. They only wanted to look for gold. But there was no gold to be found on the island.

Columbus had to send back to Spain for more food and supplies. He felt bad because he didn't have any gold to send to King Ferdinand and Queen Isabella, as he had promised. His ships couldn't even take back enough to pay for their trip!

Columbus sent twelve ships back with letters asking for more provisions. He was so desperate to prove his trip had not been a big loss to Spain that he packed the ships with goods found on the island—cinnamon, pepper, and sandalwood. But these were all of poor quality.

While the twelve ships set sail for Spain, Columbus searched for gold on other islands. He found no gold mines. Nor did he find any proof that he was really in the Indies. Columbus was not interested in finding "new" lands. He just wanted to believe that he had found the ancient lands of Marco Polo's travels.

In fact, some historians wonder if Columbus was becoming unstable. He was so obsessed with finding the Indies and finding gold that he kept refusing to face facts. He insisted he had found China and Japan. He even made his crew sign a paper, swearing that they had found the Indies!

Columbus was also beginning to suffer from a disease that would stay with him for the rest of his life. It was a form of gout that caused him great pain and made him sleep a lot.

Columbus spent five months sailing among the islands, looking for gold. Finally he became so ill that he was forced to return to the settlement of Isabella.

Columbus was so weak when he arrived that his men had to carry him off his ship. But a happy surprise was waiting for him in Isabella—his brother Bartholomew!

Columbus was overjoyed to see his brother. They had not seen each other for six years. Bartholomew had been in France when Columbus sailed away in 1492. The news of Columbus's trip took a long time to reach Bartholomew. When he finally heard, he rushed to Spain, but he had just missed the second voyage, too! Soon after he went to see King Ferdinand and Queen Isabella. They gave Bartholomew three ships filled with supplies to take to Columbus.

Now Bartholomew was in Isabella, and he was never to leave his brother's side again. Columbus was so happy to see Bartholomew that he made him governor of Isabella.

This made some of the Spaniards very jealous and resentful. In fact, they were so angry that they stole Bartholomew's three ships and sailed back to Spain! There they complained to Ferdinand and Isabella. They said that Columbus had lied—there was no gold on the islands! And they said that Columbus was acting as if he were king of the Indies.

Meanwhile, Bartholomew and Columbus were facing many problems in Hispaniola. The settlers were almost at war with the natives. The natives had grown tired of looking for gold for the Spaniards. When they put up resistance, violence followed. Bartholomew told Columbus he should be harder on the Indians—and so did a Spanish priest who was in Isabella. The priest said that Columbus was too soft with the natives. He said they were "outside Christ's law," and therefore were not brothers.

Columbus and Bartholomew decided to march against the natives to punish them. In the mountains the Spaniards met up with a great number of Indians. One historian says that there were at least ten thousand! But the Spaniards were on horses and had crossbows. So it was no contest; they won the fight. Many of the Indians had never seen horses before. Some of them thought the rider and the horse were all one animal!

The fighting between the Spaniards and Indians went on for the next ten months. The Indians raided the food depots and lay ambushes for the Spanish.

But Bartholomew made Columbus persevere and punish the natives. In a book later written by one of Columbus's sons, it was said that the Indians were finally put under control. The book said a Spaniard could finally go "wherever he pleased, enjoy the products of the soil ... and have natives carry him on their shoulders for as far as he should so desire."

During all the fighting, hundreds of natives were captured by the Spaniards. Since Columbus felt despair and disappointment about not finding gold in the Indies, he decided to be like the African explorers and try to sell these Indians as slaves.

In those days many people thought it was all right to treat non-Christians as slaves. By this time Columbus believed the Indians were heathen cannibals, so he did not seem to feel guilty when he forced five hundred of them to go to Spain to be sold as slaves. At least two hundred Indians died on the trip, and nearly all the rest died after arriving in Spain. It was said that "the country did not agree with them. . . ."

This terrible treatment of the Indians was Columbus's real downfall. He was an excellent sea commander—one of the best who ever lived. But when he tried to be a colony builder, he did not seem to know what he was doing. He was not wise about how to treat other people.

And Columbus was blinded by his quest for gold! After he had sent his shipload of natives back to be slaves, he ordered the remaining Indian men on Isabella to each fill a small bell with gold dust every three months. If they didn't find enough gold, the natives were cruelly punished.

Between 1494 and 1496 one third of the natives of Hispaniola died at the hands of the Spanish explorers.

The Admiral in Chains

IN MARCH 1496 COLUMBUS DECIDED TO RE-
turn to Spain. Before he left, a terrible
storm hit six ships in the harbor at Isabella,
and all but one were lost.

Columbus needed at least one other ship
to go back to Spain, so he built one from the
wreckage of the others. This was the first
ship built in the New World. Columbus
named it the *Santa Cruz* or *India*.

Columbus loaded the *India* and the *Niña*
with many native prisoners and two hundred sick and weary Spaniards. The two
ships were so crowded that only half the men
could lie down to sleep at once. The other
half had to wait their turn. The conditions
at sea were so harsh, and the men were suf-
fering from so much sickness and fatigue,
that many of them died during this crossing.

When the ships arrived in Spain, they
waved their banners. But no one came out to

greet them. There were no honors this time. And there was no cheering.

The people in Spain had heard about the trouble in the Indies. Now they made fun of Columbus. When he walked through the city, some people even called him the admiral of the mosquitoes!

Columbus could not understand why God had brought this trouble on him. He thought that maybe he needed to show God how humble he was. So he started wearing a monk's robe to prove that he was God's servant.

Wearing this plain brown robe, Columbus went to see the king and queen. Though they had heard many complaints against him, they were still nice to him. For one thing, they were afraid that Portugal might send ships to the New World, so they wanted Columbus to go back. They promised to give him more ships and three hundred men.

However, no one wanted to go with Columbus this time. The king and queen had to offer pardons to criminals to get them to sail with Columbus!

It took more than a year for Columbus to

prepare for his third trip. Some of the money for the trip came from the sale of the Indian slaves he'd brought back.

In 1498 eight ships sailed back to the New World. Five of them went straight to Hispaniola with supplies. But Columbus led the other three on a discovery trip.

After two months of exploring, Columbus sailed by the island of Trinidad near the coast of South America. Near there the three ships were almost destroyed by a tidal wave! Columbus named the place the Serpent's Mouth.

He then led his men onto the shore of South America. This was the first time Columbus had actually stepped onto a new continent, but he did not know it. He thought it was just another island.

In South America, Columbus and his men saw Indians wearing huge pearls. Later Spain would make a lot of money from these pearls. But Columbus did not pay any attention to the pearls at the time. He wanted only gold.

Columbus sailed along the coast of South America, stopping now and then. When he found rivers with fresh water, he began to think that this land was more than just an island. He decided it was the Garden of Eden from the Bible! Columbus actually believed that the Garden of Eden was part of the Indies.

Finally bad health forced Columbus to return to Hispaniola. Columbus's other brother, Diego, had recently joined Bartholomew there. And Columbus found the two of them having a terrible time trying to rule the island.

Bartholomew had tried to make the settlers happier by moving them away from Isabella to a new settlement called Santo Domingo—named after his father. But the settlers had run into trouble with the Indians, and there had been a lot of fighting. Furthermore, food was scarce, and discontent had spread among the Spaniards. In fact, a group of Spaniards led by a man named Roldán had become rebels, and they were now trying to take over the island.

The Columbus brothers tried to bring order to the island. For almost a year they fought with Roldán and his rebels. Columbus and his brothers were not good leaders, though. And many settlers returned to Spain to complain about them.

King Ferdinand and Queen Isabella finally decided to send an inspector named Bobadilla to Hispaniola. They wanted him to find out exactly what was going on. When Bobadilla arrived, he saw two Spaniards hanging from the gallows. Then he found five more Spaniards waiting to be hanged! They had all been tried as traitors and found guilty.

Bobadilla was shocked. He took control of the island. He arrested the Columbus brothers and ordered all three to be sent back to Spain. But first he wanted them put in chains! Columbus responded by saying that no one would dare lay a hand on him.

When Bobadilla asked who would like to put the chains around Columbus's wrists and ankles, no one stepped forward. A man who knew Columbus wrote, "Respect and compassion prevented those present from acting." Finally, however, Columbus's cook stepped forward and said he would do it "with an expressionless face, as though he were serving some new, dainty dish."

Later the captain of the ship that took Columbus back to Spain offered to take off the admiral's chains, but Columbus wouldn't let him. His pride had been hurt. He said that only the king and queen could give the order to remove his chains!

When Columbus arrived in Spain, he was a sad sight. The Spanish people felt bad watching the admiral drag his chains through the streets. Ferdinand and Isabella ordered the chains removed, but for many years afterward, painters depicted these scenes in their pictures.

Columbus never wore his chains again, but he kept them for the rest of his life. He even asked to be buried with them. He compared them to the cross that Jesus Christ had carried.

Columbus was in a rage about the treatment he had received. When he went to see

Ferdinand and Isabella, he demanded that Bobadilla be punished. He even wanted Bobadilla's head cut off! He demanded that he himself be returned to Hispaniola with full honor.

But Ferdinand and Isabella didn't do what Columbus wanted. They merely ordered Bobadilla to come home. Then they made another man the governor of Hispaniola.

Ferdinand and Isabella did allow Columbus to sail again, however. They still wanted to believe that he had found a way to the Indies. Columbus, of course, was certain he had. He said he just needed to find a passage on the western side of the islands—then China and Japan would not be far away!

So the king and queen gave Columbus four rickety old ships and a hundred and thirty-five men. But they told him *not* to land at Hispaniola this time. They told him *not* to bring back any natives as slaves. They told him to just look for gold, silver, and spices—and to stay out of trouble!

Columbus didn't really care what the king and queen said. He was just glad to be sailing again. In many ways he had the hopes and enthusiasm of a child. He was very cheerful about his next trip. He even called it his "High Voyage."

The High Voyage

ON MAY 9, 1502, CHRISTOPHER COLUMBUS
set out on his fourth voyage to the New
World, his "High Voyage." At first the sailing was perfect. Columbus and his men had
twenty-one days of wonderful weather. On
this trip Columbus took along his younger
son, Fernando, who was only thirteen years
old at the time. Fernando Columbus later
wrote a biography about his father called
*History of the Life and Deeds of Christopher Co-
lumbus.*

In his book Fernando wrote that Columbus was a friendly and cheerful man. If
he was mad, Columbus only said "May God
take you!" or "By San Fernando!" Fernando
also described his father as being very religious, and said that he had a beautiful hand-
writing and could draw wonderful maps.

Historians believe that not all of Fernando
Columbus's memories about his father are

true. Fernando was proud of Columbus and wanted to make him appear to be a faultless hero. Furthermore, after Columbus died, his sons struggled to get the rewards they thought the king owed them. Fernando might have tried to help their case by writing only good things about Columbus.

When the four ships got close to Hispaniola, Columbus noticed some odd things. The tide was rising. The winds were stronger. And he saw thin, wispy clouds moving quickly across the sky.

Columbus also felt a heaviness in the air. And he could feel his arthritis acting up—his bones were aching! All these signs meant one thing—a bad storm was on the way!

Columbus sent a message to the governor of Hispaniola, asking permission for him and his men to land there. Queen Isabella had ordered Columbus not to stop in Hispaniola, because she didn't want more fighting. But Columbus was afraid of the oncoming storm, and he needed to find a safe harbor for his men and ships. He also wanted to warn the governor about the storm.

Columbus's message warned the governor about the upcoming storm. He thought that none of the governor's ships should leave the island. But the governor laughed at Columbus's warning. He made fun of Columbus, calling him a fortune-teller. The island's thirty ships had been planning to sail for Spain—and the governor now told them to go ahead.

Meanwhile, Columbus and his men found safety near another island. Then, as Columbus expected, a terrible hurricane struck. The violent wind and waves dashed all the governor's ships against the shore. Within minutes almost all of them went down, and five hundred people were killed.

Two of Columbus's worst enemies died in that hurricane—one was Bobadilla, the inspector who had ordered Columbus put in chains! The other was Roldán, the leader of the rebels who had given Columbus so much trouble. The only governor's ship to arrive in Spain in good condition was the one that had carried Columbus's gold and possessions from Hispaniola! Meanwhile, Columbus's four ships survived the storm in perfect

shape. Columbus believed that God was on his side again.

Columbus sailed up and down the coast of Central America, looking for a passage to the Indies. He and his men landed on an island named Bonacca near the coast of Honduras. Here they found Indians who knew how to weave and how to make things from metal. The Indians were dressed in tunics, and they covered themselves with cotton blankets and shawls.

The Indians tried to tell Columbus there was gold to the north. But Columbus wanted to sail east, and he was too stubborn to change his plans. If he had changed his plans, he might have found the land of the Yucatán and discovered the gold of the Maya Indians.

Instead, Columbus sailed along the coast, and his ships met up with terrible winds and rain. Everything became filled with water, even the food. The men had to eat worm-filled biscuits! They ate the biscuits at night in the dark because they didn't want to see the worms.

When the weather got better, the sailors

went ashore. They saw many animals they had not seen before. They saw pumas, deer, and crocodiles.

After sailing again, the ships reached Panama. They were now actually only thirty-two miles from the Pacific Ocean.

Columbus did not realize another ocean was so close. It probably was good that he didn't find the Pacific Ocean, because if he had, he might have tried to cross it, looking for the Indies. And he and his men would never have survived the long trip.

Columbus did find some gold in Panama, however—more gold than he had found anywhere else. He thought he'd found King Solomon's mines from the Bible. But the gold was very hard to get out of the ground. Columbus built a fort so his men could stay and work to mine the gold.

One day in April 1503 twenty men were guarding the fort—along with an Irish wolf-hound. Suddenly four hundred natives attacked. The Indians had bows and arrows and spears. But the Spaniards had their weapons and the huge wolfhound helped them defend the fort, and the Indians had to retreat.

Next the Indians attacked a group of Spaniards on a nearby stream. They killed ten men, including one of Columbus's captains.

Meanwhile, Columbus was alone on a ship docked in the water. He was very sick with malaria. His high fever gave him delusions, and he stood on the deck of the ship and yelled and cried. He saw visions, and he thought God was talking to him.

But then one of Columbus's men—a brave sailor named Diego Mendez—helped the other men escape the Indians. Mendez put together a raft and took the Spaniards out to the admiral's ship. Columbus was so pleased with Mendez that he made him captain of a ship.

During their escape from the Indians, the sailors had to leave one of their ships behind. Now there were only three ships. But these ships could hardly sail. They were filled with holes made by shipworms! The sailors used pots and kettles to bail out the water. Finally a second ship had to be left behind because of the shipworms.

A terrible storm hit the last two ships. The storm raged for six days. During that time, Columbus was very ill. His joints were swollen with painful arthritis, and he still had a high fever from his malaria. The mosquitoes along the coasts were also making many other men sick with malaria.

Finally the storm passed. The crew barely made it to the island of Jamaica in their two ships. Then these ships completely came apart. So now Columbus and his men had no ships!

In spite of his sicknesses and the loss of all his ships, Columbus still had great willpower and faith. On Jamaica he ordered his men to build forts out of the wood from the two ships. Then Diego Mendez, the heroic captain, offered to take two canoes and go to Hispaniola for help. Only one other Spaniard would go with him. The rest of Mendez's crew were Indians.

Mendez's two canoes were so light and fragile, the task seemed impossible. But Mendez managed to navigate them over a very rough sea without even a compass. Some men died of thirst on the way. This canoe trip has been called one of the most daring adventures in the history of the sea.

After Mendez arrived in Hispaniola, he then traveled two hundred miles on foot till he came to the governor of the island. But the governor became fearful when he heard Mendez's story. He thought that Columbus might try to take over his rule of the island. So he delayed sending help to Columbus and his crew.

Meanwhile, Columbus and his men were having a hard time trying to survive on Jamaica. Their broken ships made a dry fort, and the Indians let them hunt and fish. But some of Columbus's men started giving him a lot of trouble. Impatient with their situation, they began stealing things from the Indians.

The Indians paid the Spaniards back by refusing to give them food. At one point Columbus devised a trick to get more food from the Indians. He knew that a total eclipse of the moon was going to happen. This meant that the moon would vanish from sight for a while. At sunset Columbus told the Indians to give the sailors more food—or God would make the moon go away.

When the moon started to vanish, the Indians rushed to Columbus. They begged him to save them. Columbus made the Indians repeat what they wanted—till the eclipse was almost over. Then he told the moon to come back.

After Columbus's trick the Indians gave the Spaniards all the food they had asked for.

Finally Columbus and his men saw the sail of a ship! After one year the governor of Hispaniola had finally decided to help the stranded Spaniards.

On June 28, 1504, Columbus and one hundred men headed to Hispaniola. When Columbus set sail for Spain soon afterward, most of his men did not go back with him. They had suffered enough. The last thing they wanted to do was go on another "High Voyage" with the admiral.

Last Days

IN SEPTEMBER 1504 COLUMBUS ARRIVED back in Spain. It had been eleven years since he had first returned from the New World. He was fifty-three years old and in very bad health. Columbus immediately wanted to see King Ferdinand and Queen Isabella. But the queen was dying, and King Ferdinand did not want Columbus to bother her.

When Isabella died a short time later, Columbus was grief-stricken. He had lost a good friend and a powerful supporter. The queen had never laughed at him. She had often talked the king into helping him. She had appreciated Columbus's sense of adventure and had shared his vision of creating a larger Christian world. Columbus's hopes and dreams seemed to die with Queen Isabella.

Columbus was so ill that he could not

even go to Queen Isabella's funeral. He was in bed with crippling arthritis. He had gout and malaria, and he was also having trouble with his eyes.

At the end of his life Columbus spent much of his time trying to collect the rewards due him. He had a great deal of money. But he also wanted the title of governor of Hispaniola. King Ferdinand finally promised to give the title to Columbus's son Diego.

In his last days Columbus tried to figure out why he had not come across more proof that he had found the lands of Marco Polo. He could not come up with the answer, for he had no idea that the world was three times larger than he believed it was. He had no idea that the ocean was twice as big as he thought it was. He had no idea that Japan was more than ten thousand miles to the west of Spain! Columbus still thought Japan was twenty-four hundred miles away.

In his last days Columbus's ailments caused his mind to wander a great deal. He imagined he was leading thousands of men in war. He imagined he was fighting for the

ancient city of Jerusalem. He even wrote the king, asking for money to carry out this battle.

On May 20, 1506, Christopher Columbus died. His two brothers, Diego and Bartholomew, were with him. His two sons, Diego and Fernando, were also with him—and so was his brave captain, Diego Mendez.

Columbus's last words were "Father, into Thy hands I commit my spirit."

Christopher Columbus was given a small funeral. No great officials were present—no kings, no princes, no bishops. Spain did not honor Columbus at his death. Few people realized what he'd really done. Few realized that the Admiral of the Ocean Sea had discovered a whole new world.

Epilogue

HOW DOES AN AUTHOR FIND OUT ABOUT A famous person who lived a long time ago? First the author might read other biographies about that person. The author might also read books that tell about the time the person lived.

Sometimes the author might come across old journals, manuscripts, or letters that were written by the famous person—or by a relative or friend of that person.

Several people who lived at the time of Columbus wrote books about him. One of them was Columbus's son Fernando. Since Columbus lived so long ago, many details about his life are not absolutely certain, though. Even the book written by his son Fernando is believed to be made up in some parts.

Another man who knew Columbus is considered to be a more reliable source of information. His name was Bishop Bartolome de Las Casas. Las Casas found a journal written by Columbus on his first voyage. And Las Casas put parts of that journal in his book about Columbus. At this writing the original journal has never been found. Maybe someday it will be. Then we will learn even more about the Admiral of the Ocean Sea.

Timetable of Events in the Life of
CHRISTOPHER COLUMBUS

1451 Christopher Columbus is born in Genoa, Italy.

1453 Moslem Turks take Constantinople and close off traders' overland route to Indies through Turkey.

1476 Columbus arrives in Lisbon, Portugal, and works in a map store with his brother, Bartholomew.

1480 Columbus's son, Diego, is born to Dona Felipa, his wife.

1484 Columbus asks King John II of Portugal to help him make a trip across Western Ocean to find Indies.

1484 Columbus's wife dies.

1485 Columbus takes his son, Diego, to the La Rábida monastery in Palos, Spain.

1486 Columbus has his first meeting with Queen Isabella and King Ferdinand in Cordoba, Spain, and asks them for ships and men to travel across Western Ocean.

1488 Columbus's second son, Fernando, is born to Beatrice Enriquez de Harana.

1492 In January Spain wins its long war against the Moors in Granada.

In April Queen Isabella and King Ferdinand finally agree to help Columbus.

In August Columbus sets sail with three ships and crew of ninety from Palos, Spain.

Columbus and his crew set foot on island of San Salvador in October.

In December Columbus's largest ship, the *Santa María*, sinks.

1493 Columbus arrives back in Palos, Spain, in March.

1493 In October Columbus sets sail again for the New World, this time with seventeen ships and twelve hundred men.

1496 Columbus returns to Spain in June.

1498 In May Columbus sets sail on his third voyage to the New World.

1500 In October Columbus returns to Spain in chains.

1502 In May Columbus sets out on his

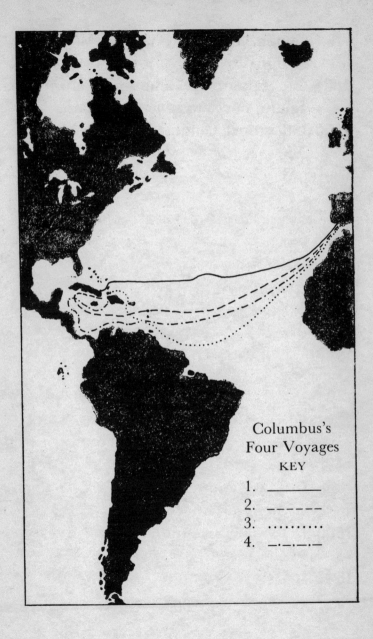

Columbus's
Four Voyages
KEY

1. —————
2. — — — — —
3. ··········
4. —·—·—·—

fourth voyage to the New World, his
"High Voyage."

1504 In September Columbus returns to
Spain, never to sail away again.

1506 Christoper Columbus dies in May.